Seymour Simon

SEE MORE READERS

GIANT SNAKES

chronicle books · san francisco

To my son Mike, who loved giant snakes when he was 10

Permission to use the following photographs is gratefully acknowledged:
Front cover: © A. B. Sheldon/Dembinsky Photo Associates; title page: © Art Wolfe/Photo Researchers, Inc.; pages 2–3, 4–5, 8–9, 28–29, and back cover: © Joe McDonald/Animals Animals; pages 6–7: © John Mitchell/Photo Researchers, Inc.; pages 10–11: © Robert Winslow/AnimalsAnimals; pages 12–13: © Michael Fogden/AnimalsAnimals; pages 14–15: © Gregory G. Dimijian/Photo Researchers, Inc.; pages 16–17: © Jan Lindblad/Photo Researchers, Inc.; pages 18 and 32: © Steve Cooper/Photo Researchers, Inc.; pages 20–21: © E. R. Degginger/Photo Researchers, Inc.; pages 22–23 and cover spot: © Renee Lynn/Photo Researchers, Inc.; pages 24–25: © Fred Voetsch/Acclaim Images; pages 26–27: © David M. Schlesser/Photo Researchers, Inc.; pages 30–31: © Jany Sanvanet/Photo Researchers, Inc.

The author especially thanks David Reuther and Ellen Friedman for their thoughtful editorial and design suggestions as well as their enthusiasm for the SeeMore Readers. Also, many thanks to Victoria Rock, Beth Weber, Molly Glover, Tracy Johnson, and Nancy Tran at Chronicle Books for their generous assistance and their support of these books.

Book design by Ellen Friedman.
Typeset in 18-point ITC Century Book.
Manufactured in China.

Library of Congress Cataloging-in-Publication Data
Simon, Seymour.
Giant snakes / Seymour Simon.
p. cm. — (SeeMore readers)
ISBN-13: 978-0-8118-5410-8 (library edition)
ISBN-10: 0-8118-5410-8 (library edition)
ISBN-13: 978-0-8118-5411-5 (pbk.)
ISBN-10: 0-8118-5411-6 (pbk.)
1. Snakes—Juvenile literature. I. Title.
QL666.O6S454 2006
597.96'7—dc22
2005025360

Distributed in Canada by Raincoast Books
9050 Shaughnessy Street, Vancouver, British Columbia V6P 6E5

10 9 8 7 6 5 4 3 2 1

Chronicle Books LLC
85 Second Street, San Francisco, California 94105

www.chroniclekids.com

Most boa constrictors are about as long
as a car.
But this boa, the anaconda, is about as
long as a school bus.

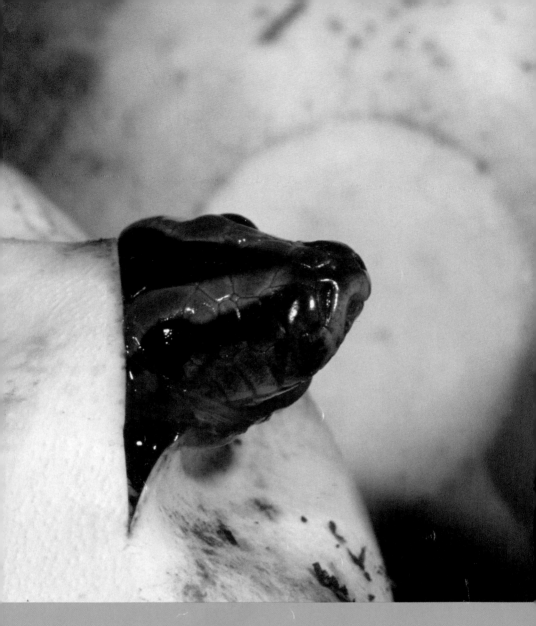

Giant snakes are either boas or pythons.
They all look much alike.
The main difference is that boas bear
living young, while pythons lay eggs.

Most boas live in South America and
Central America.
Most pythons live in Africa, India, and
Southeast Asia.

Giant snakes are the longest land animals alive today. They are even longer than an elephant or a giraffe.

Giant snakes use their flexible bodies to throw tightening coils around their prey. Giant snakes don't crush their prey. The trapped animal cannot breathe and dies of suffocation in a few minutes.

A snake can swallow an animal much larger than the snake's head. By opening its double-hinged jaws, a giant snake can make a meal of almost any animal it finds.

It can eat rats, lizards, and birds.
It can even eat deer, monkeys, and pigs.
Giant snakes may also feed on domestic
animals such as sheep, goats, chickens,
and dogs.

Some giant snakes wait in trees or on rocky ledges for their prey to pass below. Other giant snakes hunt by crawling into holes and burrows where animals may be hiding.

Snakes that live in water go after fish,
turtles, and young alligators or crocodiles.
Giant snakes can fast for a long time
between feedings.
Some snakes eat only three or four good
meals a year.

All the giant snakes live
in warm places.
Giant snakes depend on
sunlight, warm air, or
sun-warmed surfaces
to keep warm.
They become cold if
their surroundings
are cold.
Snakes are called
cold-blooded
animals, meaning they
get heat from their
surroundings.
Mammals and birds are
called warm-blooded
because their bodies
produce heat.

Giant snakes have no outside ears and probably cannot hear sounds very well, though they can sense vibrations through the ground.
They find prey even at night, mostly through smell and through heat-sensitive pits in the lower jaw.

Giant snakes see well underwater
because of clear, watertight coverings
over their eyes.
In fact, snakes cannot close their eyes
or blink.

Anacondas are the largest snakes
in the world.
They are found in the tropical parts of
South America and Central America.
Anacondas may reach lengths of nearly 30
feet, measure over 12 inches in diameter,
and weigh over 500 pounds.

A female anaconda can give birth to
20 to 40 or more live babies, each about
2 feet long.

The anaconda babies can swim, hunt,
and care for themselves within hours
after birth.

The reticulated (re-TICK-u-late-d)
python of Southeast Asia is the longest
snake in the world.
The record length for this python
is nearly 33 feet, with a weight of
over 300 pounds.
One of the most beautiful of all
the snakes, the reticulated python
is a favorite in zoos and circuses.
It is a good swimmer and hunts near
rivers and lakes.
Some have even been found swimming
far out at sea.
Female pythons lay 25 to 80 large,
white eggs and coil around the eggs to
brood them for 80 to 90 days.
The mother python will defend her
eggs, but once the babies are born,
they are on their own.

The largest African pythons are close to 30 feet long, but most grow only to between 15 and 20 feet. This python is the only giant African snake.

It's home is in grasslands, forests, farmlands, mountains, lakes, and rivers, but not in the great deserts.

This python is a good swimmer and can go far from land.

It often climbs trees and hunts for birds, monkeys, and other prey among the branches.

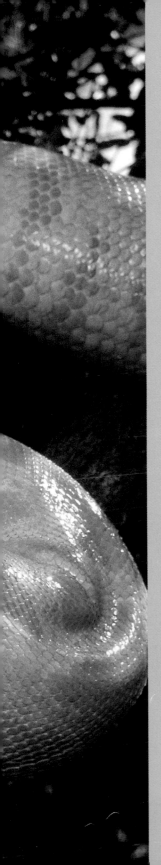

The Indian python is a favorite
giant snake in circuses,
carnivals, and snake shows.
Indian pythons often wrap
their bodies around their
human handlers and squeeze
tight.

Some handlers say that if the
snake is less than 12 or 13 feet
long, there is no need to worry!
Most Indian pythons are
between 10 and 15 feet long,
and none are longer than 21 feet.
The Indian python lives in
Pakistan, India, Sri Lanka, and
parts of China.

The amethystine (am-e-THIS-tine) python is thinner than any of the other giant snakes. The snake gets its name from scales that have a purple or blue shine that looks like a gem called the amethyst (am-e-THIS-t). This python lives in Australia and some of the nearby islands. It eats prey such as small rodents, birds, and lizards. It also eats chickens and other domestic animals.

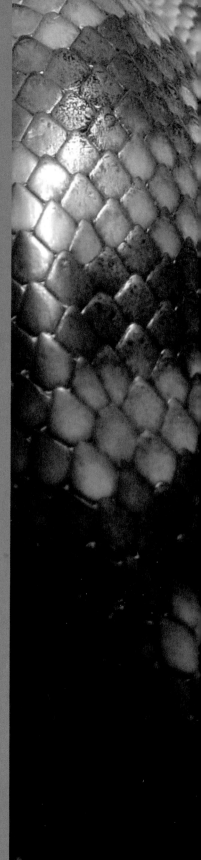

The boa
constrictor is
the smallest
of the six giant
snakes.
Most boas are
less than 10 feet
long, and the
record length
is about 15 feet.
Boas are found
in Mexico,
Central America,
and South
America.
They mainly eat
birds and small
mammals such
as rats.

Giant snakes rarely attack people. One reason is that most people are just too big to be eaten, even by a giant snake. Snakes mostly avoid people, and those that do attack a person are usually killed. The fact that there are so few stories about giant-snake attacks shows how rare they really are.

People are the worst enemies of giant snakes.

Not only do many people kill any giant snake they see, but they also hunt snakes for their skins and meat.

And when people build new cities and roads, there is less room for giant snakes to live and to find the foods they need.

When giant snakes are first born or hatched, they have many other enemies such as mammals, lizards, birds, and even other snakes.

By the time a giant snake is over 10 feet long, very few animals will attack it. Tigers and other big cats sometimes attack giant snakes, but battles with elephants, bears, and sharks are just made-up tales or have been staged by people.

Giant snakes are neither good nor bad.
Giant snakes are part of the natural life
of the countries in which they live.